DINEFWR CASTLE

Rob Gittins

Gomer Press
1984

First Impression - May 1984

ISBN 0 86383 032 3

Printed by J. D. Lewis and Sons Ltd., Gomer Press, Llandysul

CONTENTS

ACKNOWLEDGEMENTS

All photographs in this volume are reproduced by kind permission of Roger Vlitos. The map of Dinefwr Castle was prepared by Dorian Spencer Davies.

The windy summit wild and high
Rushing roughly on the sky
The pleasant seat and ruin'd tower
The naked rock and shady bower

John Dyer on Dinefwr Castle in *'Grongar Hill'*.

The publication of this concise history and description of Dinefwr Castle, illustrated by Mr. Roger Vlitos' fine photographs, is a most valuable service which puts us in debt to Mr. Rob Gittins.

Although it has been so shamefully ignored and neglected, Dinefwr which was built by the Welsh, is historically the most important of all the castles of Wales. Generations before the great Edwardian castles were raised to hold the Welsh down, Dinefwr was built to defend them. It was the seat of Welsh government 150 years before Caernarfon, for example, was built; but whereas the Government has maintained Caernarfon and many others in splendid condition, so that their visitors are reckoned in hundreds of thousands, decaying Dinefwr is visited by no more than a score or so in a year.

The greatest man associated with Dinefwr is Rhys ap Gruffydd, who, in the last third of the twelfth century, was the outstanding prince in Wales. It is not too much to say that but for his heroic and successful struggle there would be little more than faint traces of the national language and identity of Wales in Dyfed today. His memory should be honoured, as that of his ancestor Hywel Dda now is, by a worthy memorial. And what better site for this than in or near Dinefwr Castle?

The possibilities of Dinefwr are indeed impressive. Not only has it the advantage of unique historical importance, it is also magnificently sited. Placed on a wooded bluff overlooking the verdant beauty of the Tywi valley to the south and the glorious park designed by Capability Brown to the north, it could be the most attractive historical site in Wales, drawing scores of thousands annually to visit it.

And there will be more to see than the great vista and the main castle structure. Surrounding the castle there is a large area which calls for careful archaeological work which is sure to yield fascinating results. It may be found that Dinefwr has been a military site through the early Middle ages back to the Roman period and even before that. This rich history should be set out, and the artefacts found during the excavations should be exhibited, in a well designed building conveniently situated. The interest and educational value of the exhibition will itself be a magnet attracting visitors.

Such a complex would obviously be of immense economic advantage to the neighbourhood and would add substantially to the attractions of Dyfed. In particular it would put Llandeilo on the tourist map. And of course the work to be done on this major project would give employment.

But will the Welsh Office, which has responsibility for ancient monuments in Wales come up to scratch? In the past it was uninterested. It has taken no initiative in the matter. In 1977, under pressure, it did at last agree to take Dinefwr over and do its duty by it. But it was not until early 1983, after further heavy pressure, that it began to move to some effect. Clearance work began that summer. But in the autumn of 1983 I had a dispiriting letter from Mr. Wyn Roberts M.P. of the Welsh Office, saying that the castle would not be in a condition to admit the public for 10 years! And the access road, which is so essential, will not be built until the end of that period. This is unacceptable. The Government should have done the job scores of years ago. Now that it has so tardily started, one has a right to hope that it will accept the challenge with enthusiasm and complete the work in five years.

Gwynfor Evans

Dinefwr Castle was one of the most import-ant locations of ancient Wales. It housed many of Wales' greatest leaders including the legendary Lord Rhys and was the capital of Wales' ancient southern kingdom of Deheu-barth. In this role it acted as one of the main nodal points of Welsh resistance to foreign invasion.

The setting of Dinefwr Castle still recalls the majesty of former times. From the southern aspect the ruined castle commands the broad sweep of the Tywi valley while from the more accessible northern approach-es the castle stands as it has for centuries; imposing among the dense trees. Dinefwr retains the atmosphere of former glories and is one of the most evocative of all Welsh castles.

The design of Dinefwr also provides a fasci-nating insight into changes in castle design. The remains of the earliest motte and bailey system are still discernible as are the more sophisticated defensive arrangements of the Norman and Edwardian eras and the sumpt-uous domestic developments of the later Middle ages. The ruin of Dinefwr Castle records all these architectural changes and provides a valuable insight into the many and varied developments in military thought.

There are few castles more important to an understanding of Welsh history than Dinefwr or more atmospheric in its stark and inac-cessible setting. Dinefwr is one of the most ignored but most valuable of all Welsh castles.

The Tywi valley viewed from the twelfth century keep.

The origins of Dinefwr Castle are shrouded in mystery. The name 'Dinefwr' is thought to mean 'Dinas Ifor', Fortress of Ifor after Ifor ab Alun, reputedly an incumbent of Dinefwr in 683 AD, although it is possible that the name may also mean 'Ebor's fort', named after the Bishop Ebur, another incumbent of the fortress in 314 AD.[1] Yet another source suggests that 'Efwr's fort' was so-named because of the profusion of 'Efwr' or cow parsnips that grow around the castle slopes.[2]

The date of the castle's construction is similarly obscure. Roman finds discovered in the vicinity indicate that the site was in active use as a Roman hill fort long before a castle was constructed on the site. The lines of the early entrenchments are still visible around the present ruin and clearly indicate a primitive hill fort. Precisely when a castle superseded the early hill fortification, however, is unclear. The first written evidence for the existence of Dinefwr Castle is in the *Book of Llandaff.* This book refers to the site when the seventh century king of Dyfed, Noe ab Arthur, gave the land of Llandeilo Fawr to the diocese of Llandaff which then became the centre of a powerful religious community (a 'clas'). Dinefwr is mentioned by Gerallt Gymro (Giraldus Cambrensis) four centuries later as one of the principal courts of Wales, but its name does not appear in *The Mabinogion* where one might expect to find it accorded some prominence. The earliest reference in *The Chronicles* to Dinefwr is not made until the year 1162, although it is then mentioned in a way that indicates it was already a well-known and powerful fortress.

It is most likely that Dinefwr Castle was constructed by Rhodri Fawr (Rhodri the Great) about 856 AD, probably in direct response to the Viking invasion of Wales. Wales had suffered various invasions since the Roman occupation of AD 49. Pict and Saxon invaders attacked Wales in 490 AD only to be driven out by the legendary Welsh figure of Arthur. But then, in 851 AD, Danish

Vikings attempted an attack along Wales' sparsely defended west coast, and the great Welsh leader Rhodri rose to defeat the Viking aggressors. On driving the Viking invaders from his country Rhodri seized the initiative offered by the general peace and created a united Wales under his rule. It was at this time that Rhodri most probably constructed his own castle at Dinefwr. Thus Dinefwr, long a site of some influence, became one of the great centres of early Wales.

Rhodri died in 878 AD. To prevent wrangling among his successors, Rhodri split Wales into three large kingdoms, Gwynedd in the north, Powys in mid-Wales and Deheubarth in the south. Rhodri's second son Cadell was installed into Dinefwr to control the southern kingdom of Deheubarth, but Cadell is now eclipsed in Welsh history by the rise of *his* more famous son, Hywel Dda.

Hywel Dda became the most famous of all Welsh kings, out-shining even Rhodri Fawr in fame and renown. The *Brut y Tywysogion* calls him the 'head and glory of all the Britons' and Hywel Dda became the most glittering Welsh leader associated with Dinefwr. By 950 AD he was minting coinage depicting himself enthroned as head of State over Wales and Wessex, and Dinefwr flourished as the major seat of this new Welsh king. When Hywel Dda formulated his famous Welsh law—the law which involved the tenth century king in travels to Rome—it was stipulated that a statutory copy be deposited at Dinefwr. This law, *Cyfraith Hywel*, had a far reaching effect on the evolution of Welsh history. Its major features survive to this day and give a vivid account of a humane and just form of early administration.

On Hywel Dda's death the line of Welsh Kings at Dinefwr passed to Rhys ap Tewdwr. Rhys, however, was destined to be the last king of Wales for within a few years of the commencement of his rule, Wales suffered its most devastating invasion. Dinefwr was soon to lose pride of place as the effective centre of early, independent Wales.

In 1067 the Normans, having previously conquered the English, began to drive into

[1] See *Archaeologia Cambrensis*, 1925, p. 457.
[2] ibid., p. 458.

Wales. The Welsh kingdom of Deheubarth strenuously held out against the Norman invaders with the royal line of Dinefwr active in the spirited resistance, but the Normans proved too strong for Deheubarth. Dinefwr and the rest of Wales now passed under the control of a foreign power. On their assumption of power the Normans began to organise their captured lands into lordships and to use their coastal castles at Cardigan, Pembroke and Carmarthen as the nodal points of the new Norman kingdom. From these bases the Normans inexorably tightened their grip on the interior of the country.

But if Dinefwr could not resist the Normans in military strength, the castle did house one Welsh 'weapon' that was to wreak havoc among the foreign intruders. Rhys' daughter, the Princess Nest, was by all contemporary accounts, one of the most beautiful women Wales has ever seen. Contemporary bards record that when Princess Nest walked in Dinefwr's grounds in her childhood, men would hide behind bushes for days just to catch a glimpse of her.

After the capture of Dinefwr, the princess was given in reward to the Norman castellan of Pembroke, Gerald de Windsor. However, his Norman King, Henry I, also fell in love with her after a visit to Dinefwr, although the princess appears to have rejected both men as she eloped with the son of the ruler of Ceredigion and Powys, Owain ap Cadwgan. Gerald de Windsor pursued the two lovers across Wales, eventually capturing ap Cadwgan and killing him. He failed however to capture the princess' undivided love as she went on to bear a child by Henry I himself, a son who was to be killed in battle at Anglesey. Her legitimate daughter Angharad was to become mother of the famed Gerallt Gymro. Dinefwr never saw a woman like the Princess Nest again. The kings of Wales left a remarkable woman behind them.

On the wider military front the Norman peace in Wales was always an uneasy one and, in response to the charged atmosphere in the country, yet another great Welsh leader was now emerging to threaten directly the Normans. This leader was once more based at Dinefwr and was directly descended from the line of Welsh princes. His name was Rhys ap Gruffydd.

This new Lord of Dinefwr, Rhys, was left an orphan at the age of 5 when his mother Gwenllian was killed leading an attack on Cydweli (Kidwelly). A field near Cydweli town centre is still named Maes Gwenllian to this day. From his mother Rhys derived his spirit of resistance and independence and his willingness to serve the independent Welsh cause. The death of Henry I in 1135 gave the new rising prince the opportunity he craved.

In the wake of the wrangling for the English throne, Rhys began to drive against the uncertain Norman strongholds in the south. He was joined by Owain Gwynedd who similarly began to move against the Normans in the north of Wales. Henry II, acceding to the English throne in 1154, marshalled a huge army to stamp out Welsh insurrection and crossed the country to meet the combined forces of Owain Gwynedd of North Wales, Rhys ap Gruffydd of Deheubarth and Owain Cyfeiliog of Powys. The result was an historic victory for the Welsh.

The Lord Rhys who now came to preside over an independent Deheubarth has become a rightly renowned figure in Welsh history. He was a formidable man, who in his 50-year reign regained most of the Welsh lands lost to the Normans and built new defensive fortifications the length and breadth of his kingdom. But Rhys was not only a warrior and nor did he triumph merely by his military skill, he also united his southern kingdom under his rule. Gerallt Gymro, the narrator, tells the story of the continuing battles between Henry II and Lord Rhys in 1162, when Henry despatched a messenger from his camp in Wales to assess the practicality of an attack upon Dinefwr. This messenger was:

> . . . a soldier born in Bretagne on whose wisdom and conduct he could rely, under the conduct of Gwaedden, Dean of Cantref Mawr, to explore the situation of Dinefor Castle and the strength of the country. The priest, although desired to take the soldier by the easiest and best road to the castle, led him purposely aside by the most difficult and inaccessible paths and whenever they passed through woods the priest, to the general surprise of all present, fed upon grass asserting that in times of need the inhabitants of that country were accustomed to live upon herbs and roots. The soldier, returning to the King and relating what had happened affirmed that the country was uninhabitable, vile and

inaccessible and scarcely affording food to a beastly nation living like brutes.

King Henry did not attack Dinefwr!

Rhys was also a famed patron of the arts, perhaps the most influential in Welsh history. In 1176 Rhys called together at Cardigan Castle Wales' first-ever National Eisteddfod, the Welsh celebration that persists to this day.

Lord Rhys remained active to the end. In 1195, perhaps counting on the prince's maturity of years, two members of his family, Rhys Grug and Maredudd, attempted to seize power but even in his 60s the Lord Rhys proved more than a match for them. He captured the two rebels and shut them away in the castle of Ystrad Meurig in Ceredigion. The next year, as if to prove his prevailing power, Rhys went on the warpath attacking Carmarthen Castle which had long been a thorn in his side. He burnt the town to the ground, subjugating many of his old enemies in the area and confirming the southern kingdom of Deheubarth under his rule.

The great Lord Rhys of Dinefwr died in 1197. He had presided over his ancient ancestral seat for over fifty years. At the time of his death, Rhys was in fact under excommunication but by an arrangement with the Bishop Peter he was given a Christian burial in St David's and it was a fitting resting place for the Welsh ruler. No prince did more for South Wales and its independence than the Lord Rhys and this prince, in all the chronicles, is portrayed as a paragon of all the princely virtues and hailed as the one defender of Wales.

But the earlier rising by members of Rhys' family presaged bitter dynastic struggles and these exploded after the prince's death. Under the Welsh law formulated by Hywel Dda and kept at Dinefwr, each of Rhys' sons were entitled to a portion of his land, a prize made infinitely richer by the new and hard-won independence of the Welsh land. Although Rhys had made an attempt to apportion the castles in his kingdom among his family, these efforts to satisfy their warring ambitions were swept aside immediately after his death. Eventually, in 1204 his son Rhys Grug came to control Dinefwr.

Rhys Grug maintained in full the vigorous and boisterous rule established by his father.

He emulated all his illustrious ancestor's aggression although he did not demonstrate his father's political judgement. Rhys Grug, from his base at Dinefwr, took on all the Norman castles on Gower and actually burnt the town of Swansea to the ground. He also took the castles at Cydweli, Llanymddyfri (Llandovery) and Llangadog. But his hold on Dinefwr was always tenuous and he was soon under seige in the castle from his own brother Rhys Ieuanc (Rhys the Younger). Rhys Grug suffered defeat but recaptured the castle a few years later. Rhys was eventually killed in characteristic fashion leading an attack on Carmarthen Castle. He came under fire from a fleet sailing up the Tywi river and was fatally wounded. Rhys was carried back to Dinefwr (even though it may then have been occupied by another Welsh ruler), where he was attended by Rhiwallon, the first of the Physicians of Myddfai, son of the Lady of the Lake. But Rhys died and was buried, like his father before him, with full honours at St David's.

While the immediate attention around Dinefwr was focused on these dynastic battles for supremacy, far more important movements were taking place in the Welsh world. Wales was now witnessing the rise of the greatest of all Welsh princes, rivalling the great Lord Rhys himself in military skill and political awareness; Llewelyn ap Iorwerth or Llewelyn Fawr (Llewelyn the Great). In the wake of the Welsh victories over Henry II, Llewelyn rose as leader of Gwynedd but soon began extending his influence over an increasing area of Wales while the then English king—Richard I (The Lionheart)— was away on the Crusades. It was not long before Llewelyn came into contact with Rhys Grug and the dynasty of Dinefwr. Rhys did not take this outside influence lightly even from as great a leader as Llewelyn. First the Dinefwr prince burnt the town of Llandeilo so that it would not afford succour to Llewelyn and then he actually dismantled Dinefwr Castle in order that it should not provide a base for the intruder. Soon however Llewelyn had prevailed upon the remaining skeleton garrison to surrender and had installed his own men into the castle. Dinefwr was quickly restored and for the rest of the great Llewelyn's reign, Dinefwr Castle settled under his rule.

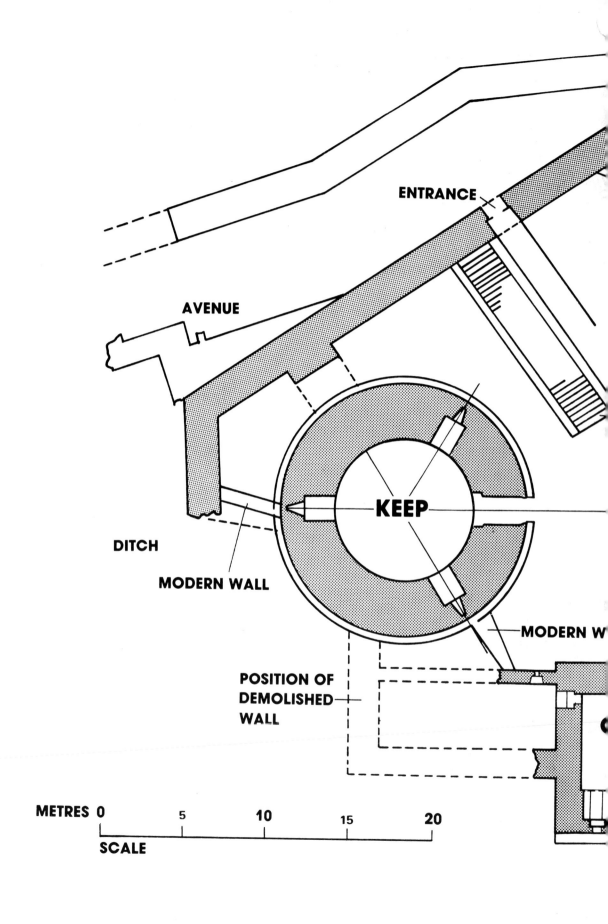

ENTRANCE

AVENUE

KEEP

DITCH

MODERN WALL

MODERN W

POSITION OF
DEMOLISHED
WALL

METRES 0   5   10   15   20

SCALE

DINEFWR CASTLE

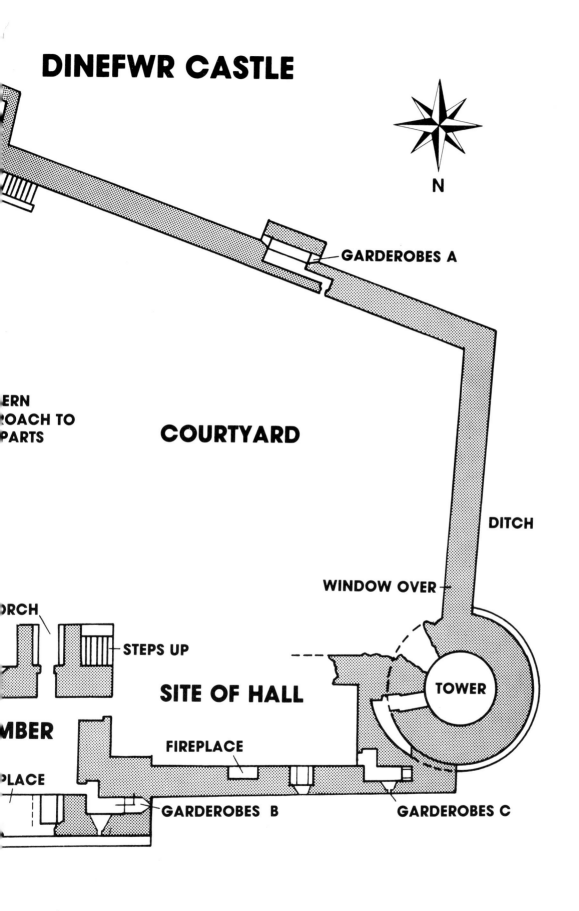

N

GARDEROBES A

ERN
ROACH TO
PARTS

COURTYARD

DITCH

WINDOW OVER

ORCH

STEPS UP

SITE OF HALL

TOWER

MBER

FIREPLACE

PLACE

GARDEROBES B

GARDEROBES C

When Llewelyn died in 1240 however, he left no clear successor. In the event his grandson Llewelyn ap Gruffydd came to power. The younger Llewelyn immediately styled himself 'Prince of Wales' and set about securing formal recognition of Welsh independence from England. This he achieved in the Treaty of Montgomery in 1258. Llewelyn had installed Rhys Fychan into Dinefwr in 1255 but ejected him in favour of his close relation Maredudd in 1257. But Llewelyn did not show the same strong purpose as his grandfather and in less than two years the custody of Dinefwr changed again when Llewelyn ejected Maredudd, and once again installed Rhys Fychan. This lack of a consistent purpose was to be Llewelyn's downfall.

As Llewelyn fought to hold on to his kingdom a new English king was rising against insurrection in his kingdom. The new king, Edward I, was determined to rule the whole of Britain from an English base once more. Llewelyn's grandson was soon to be tested to the full and the enemies he had made in his indecision over the gift of Dinefwr were to cost him dearly.

In 1277, five years after his accession, Edward marched into Wales at the head of a great army, determined to subjugate the land once more. Maredudd, ejected from Dinefwr, now began to plot with the English King and in return he was promised the stronghold of Dinefwr on the present incumbent's defeat. Within twelve months Edward was deep into South Wales and late in 1277 his forces began advancing up the Tywi valley from Cydweli and their captured stronghold at Cydweli Castle. Soon they arrived at Dinefwr Castle and, with the help of the local knowledge of Maredudd, captured the stronghold of Deheubarth. Rhys was forced into submiss-

ion and empowered to attend a nearby field conference with Edward's chief general, Pain de Cadurcis. At this conference six Welsh noblemen were killed on the spot. Faced with this intimidation Rhys gave up the castle of Dinefwr to the English and never again did the castle return to the line of South Wales. Within the next few months the rest of Wales was similarly under Edward's control.

Edward set about installing his own men into the captured Welsh castles and now appears to have reneged on his promise to install Maredudd into Dinefwr. The British Record Office holds a notice of a parliamentary petition, No. 3122, which dates from the early reign of Edward 1. It is a petition to the king and his council by Maredudd averring that Dinefwr belonged to Maredudd as of right and had been promised to him by King Edward and Pain de Cadurcis on its capture from his kinsmen. Maredudd complained that this promise had not been fulfilled. He was, however, a little too vocal in his complaints for in 1291 the savagely ruthless Edward swiftly silenced his opposition by executing him as a rebel. The Constable of Carreg Cennen, John Giffard, was made Constable of Dinefwr in 1290 and charged with its upkeep, although this trusteeship was changed from Giffard to Walter de Pederton in 1297.

But Edward still had other isolated instances of unrest to face in Wales. In 1283 Llewelyn's brother Dafydd seized Hawarden Castle and sent a spirit of revolt running through the country. Edward's defences however proved too secure. Dafydd was captured and hung drawn and quartered in Shrewsbury while one year earlier Llewelyn himself was killed in an ambush by a party of English soldiers near Cilmeri on the outskirts of Builth Wells. There is also a record that Dinefwr itself was burned in 1316 by those who took part in another rebellion with another Welsh leader, Llewelyn Bren, but this seems to have been an isolated incident. The contemporary constable, Edmund Hakelut, was provided with men and money to deal with the rising which was easily crushed. In 1338, perhaps connected with this burning, repairs were ordered to Dinefwr and the castle, like the rest of Wales, settled down to a period of general peace that was to last nearly one hundred years.

Dinefwr's *domestic* life now came briefly to the fore. An eloquent portrait of this domestic activity is painted in the Rent Assize record and the Court Roll for 1302/13. Around the castle grew a small community of 13 houses which squatted under the castle walls. In this community a fishery was operated from the Tywi by one Harry Scurlages who was also tenant of the local mill. Salmon were sold in Dinefwr for 10d each, and a local miller Hugh le Mailer sold flour. This close-knit community ushered in a period of domestic stability around the castle but it was not to persist for long. Dinefwr was soon to become the subject of a fierce *internal* dispute.

The strong Edward I was succeeded on his death by the weak and pliable Edward II. In Wales, Edward soon fell under the influence of the hated Welsh baron Hugh Despenser who fast acquired extensive territories in the country through his influence over the uncertain English King. Edmund Hakelut was still Constable of Dinefwr at this time but in 1318 Despenser received the castle after the King had picked a quarrel with Hakelut. To the noblemen of Wales this was just one more outrageous act on Despenser's part, but their full fury was aroused three years later in 1321 when the power-thirsty baron attempted to annex by force the Lordship of Gower. It was an unfortunate miscalculation on Despenser's part. The other lords of South Wales rose against him destroying Dinefwr Castle in the process. Although Edward was forced to side with the majority of Welsh lords however, he soon found an early opportunity to welcome Despenser back into the fold and restore all his old territories. The English king engineered a dispute with the coalition of Welsh lords and sent in the English army against them. Many of the constables of Deheubarth were executed in the ensuing campaign.

But Despenser was not destined to exert his influence much longer. On Edward's death in 1325 his Queen, Isabella, aware and mistrustful of the Welsh baron, ordered his execution. Edmund Hakelut was again granted the keep of Dinefwr and was reimbursed all his arrears of constable's fees. For the rest of the century Dinefwr passed steadily and peaceably from one constable to the next. It was Dinefwr's most protracted period of peace for centuries.

But by the end of the fourteenth century, Wales was in turmoil again. In 1400 a new Welsh leader rose, once more fired by the dream of Welsh independence. His name was Owain Glyndŵr, a warrior who was to prove a worthy heir to the tradition of Rhodri, Llewelyn the Great and the Lord Rhys.

Glyndŵr's rise coincided with Henry IV's preoccupation in maintaining his tenuous grip on the English throne. The new English king was totally unprepared for the huge welling of support for the Welsh leader and totally unable to contain it. Glyndŵr began taking all the English strongholds in Wales and by 1403, the third year of his rebellion, had reached Dinefwr. The Constable of Dinefwr at this time was Jenkin Hanard and he wrote two letters from the beseiged castle to John Fairford, Receiver of Brecknock, which eloquently paint his plight. These two letters survive to this day:

> Dear Friend, I do you to writ that Owen Glyndwr, Henry Don, Rees Ddu, Rees ap Gri ap Llewellyn, Rees Gether have won the town of Carmarthen and . . . have burnt the town and slain more than fifty men, and they be in purpose to Kidwelly and a seige is ordained at the castle I keep and that is great peril for me, for they have made a vow that they will at all events have us dead therein. Wherefore I pray you not to beguile us but send to us warning shortly whether we may have any help or no and if help is not coming that we may have an answer, that we may steal away by night to Brecknock because we fail victuals and men, especially men; also Jenkin ap Llewellytn hath yielden up the castle of Emlyn with free will and also William Gwyn, and many gentles are in person with Owen . . .
>
> Written at Dynevour Castle in haste and dread on the feast of St Thomas the Martyr, Jenkin Hanard. 'Constable de Dynevour'. [3]

The above was written on Saturday, 7 July 1403. Four days later the increasingly apprehensive constable was writing again:

> Dear Friend, I do you to writ that Owen was in purpose to Kidwelly and the baron of Carew was coming with a great retinue towards St Clare and Owen changed his purpose and rode to meet the baron and that night he lodged at St Clare and destroyed all the country about and on

Tuesday they were at treaties all day and that night he lodged him at the town of Locharn six miles out of the town of Carmarthen. The intention is, if the baron of Carew and he accord in treaty then he turneth again to Carmarthen for his part of the good, and Rees Ddu his part. And many of the great masters stand yet in the castle of Carmarthen for they have not yet made their ordinance whether the castle and the town shall be burnt or no and therefore if there is any help coming haste them towards us for every house is full about of their poultry, and yet wine and honey enough in the country and wheat and beans . . .; we of the castle of Dynevour had treaties with him on Monday, Tuesday and Wednesday (9, 10 and 11 July 1403) and now he will ordain for us to leave that castle for that was the chief place in old time; and Owen's muster on Monday was eight thousand and twelve score spears (8240) such as they were. Other tidings I not now but God of Heaven send you and us from all enemies.

> Written at Dynevour this Wednesday in haste. Jenkin Hanard. [4]

Despite the constable's apprehension however, Dinefwr seems to have withstood the attack by Glyndŵr and within a few years the English king had found the measure of the Welsh rebel too. Henry Bolingbroke began to move against the Welsh strongholds in the north and east of Wales and, by 1410, had forced Glyndŵr into hiding. Glyndŵr's fate remains a mystery to this day and he simply disappeared from the Welsh scene. Welsh nationalism thus lost its last major military hero.

Dinefwr Castle rose to prominence only once more, at the end of the fifteenth century when Sir Rhys ap Thomas came to hold Dinefwr as the favourite of Henry VII. This Welsh nobleman reputedly slew Richard III at the Battle of Bosworth in 1485 and actually placed the English crown on Henry's head. He was subsequently laden with honours, his titles including that of Governor of Wales. However an ancient prophecy brought down the noble line of Rhys and also signalled the end for Dinefwr Castle. Rhys ap Thomas' grandson styled himself Rhys Griffiths Fitz-Urien and unwisely fell foul of Henry VIII's foul temper and Anne Boleyn's eager and cutting tongue. It was rumoured that Rhys Griffiths was a conspirator with James of Scotland in a plot against the English throne.

[3] See *Archaeologia Cambrensis*, 1851, pp. 114/6.

[4] ibid.

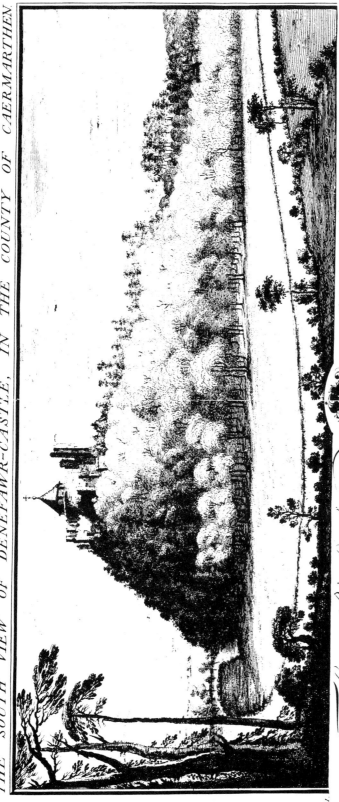

Buck's view of Dinefwr Castle, 1740.

The name FitzUrien and the Rhys family crest (the raven) also brought to Henry's mind the prophecy that the 'red hand' would take the English crown. FitzUrien was beheaded for treason in 1531 and all his property, including Dinefwr, was confiscated. Though the castle and its lands were later restored to the Rhys family, this interruption marked the end of active life for Dinefwr. Between 1595 and 1603 a house was erected nearby (the site of the present mansion) and the castle was abandoned.

Dinefwr Castle was sporadically attended to over the next few centuries, but this attention was largely cosmetic. In the late seventeenth century for example, a summer house was added on to the castle's former keep, but this soon fell, like the rest of the castle, into decay. Today, centuries later, the long protected period of neglect has proved near-catastrophic for this most famous of all Welsh castles. The tide however may soon turn. In 1983 the Welsh Office announced that they were to restore Dinefwr Castle and preserve it for the Welsh nation. Thus Dinefwr may yet rise once more to its rightful position of pride overlooking the ancient hunting grounds of Golden Grove and its former kingdom of Deheubarth.

Dinefwr Castle occupies a commanding position on the highest point of a ridge bordering the northern bank of the River Tywi. On one side a steep precipice falls hundreds of feet to the banks of the river. On the other the ground falls away in a series of gentle declivities offering excellent visibility for miles around. The castle itself is built on a narrow ledge that affords an enemy little opportunity to gain a foothold immediately outside the castle walls. The position of Dinefwr Castle was carefully chosen by its first occupants as a site practically impregnable against attack.

Dinefwr Castle consists of *two wards* side by side. The practice of building a castle inside two sets of defences owes its origin to the great period of castle-building in the late twelfth century and the reign of Edward 1. It was intended that even should an attacker overcome the first line of defence they still had to overcome the second, in the process often laying themselves open to attack in the open space between the two wards.

The *outer ward* of Dinefwr was protected principally by an earth bank and deep ditch and the *inner ward* by a curtain wall flanked by towers inside a deeper ditch defence.

The basic plan of Dinefwr Castle strongly suggests a previous *motte and bailey*, one of the earliest forms of castles in Britain. This probability is supported by references in 1282 to the 'small court tower, a kitchen, two large houses in the outer bailey, a ditch around the outer bailey and another around the castle, an ox-house in the courtyard, a minor gate and a newly-constructed draw-bridge'. In *Early Norman Castles*, G. Armitage further supports this view, suggesting that the motte was probably lowered to form the present smaller inner ward.[1] While it is not possible to date precisely the various alterations that were made to Dinefwr Castle, it is likely that this motte and bailey system was replaced in the reign of Edward I by the present, more sophisticated defensive

structure. The *main entrance* to Dinefwr Castle lay in the castle's south-east curtain wall which faces directly onto the castle's steepest precipice. This entrance fronted onto a narrow gateway, probably surmounted by a small tower. The gateway in turn led into a *narrow avenue*. At the entrance to this avenue was situated Dinefwr's *barbican*, its long stepped outwork defending the exterior of the castle. Also included at this end of the avenue was a *large triangular buttress* which narrowed access into the avenue itself. This buttress has a large deep recess at its lower point which could have been a fireplace although the apparent absence of any chimney flue indicates that it may have been a primitive form of warder's lodge. A *large gate* was fixed at this point connecting the triangular buttress with the most southerly curtain rampart. This *southern rampart* provided the castle's first line of defence from the steep southern precipice and was some thirty metres high and just under two metres thick.

On the eastern approach to Dinefwr, a *deep ditch* ran from the north to the south of the castle blocking direct access from the whole eastern side. This ditch was fourteen metres wide and extended to the very edge of the castle's southern precipice. The ditch was viaducted when it reached the entrance to the avenue and this was the location of Dinefwr's *drawbridge*. The last drawbridge into the castle was built in 1282/3 at a cost of 31s. 6d. (£1.57½)!

On the *western* approach to the castle one of Dinefwr's most remarkable features emerges; the almost total absence of defensive towers. The castle's impregnable position was clearly felt to obviate the need for such arrangements. The only such tower at Dinefwr in fact, lies in this west curtain wall.

This *tower* is entered from the castle courtyard by stairs projecting into the inner ward and is a two-storeyed structure that was probably topped by a turreted roof. The interior of the tower is three metres in diameter. A small underground apartment, two and a half metres deep was constructed under this tower and may have been a store.

[1] See Royal Commission on the Ancient and Historical Monuments and Constructions in Wales and Monmouthshire, Vol. 5, p. 108.

Evidence of stairs leading to the roof also hint at a watch turret, and stairs from this tower led to the rampart walks which probably connected with wall-walks all the way round the castle.

On the *northern* curtain wall, the northern rampart connects the castle's sole drum tower with a *watch tower* built into the north curtain wall. This would afford excellent visibility for miles to the north of Dinefwr, the aspect most likely to suffer attack. The watch tower projects high above the rest of the buildings on the north curtain. One unusual feature of the watch tower is that it contained a *well* to the left of the first landing. In the watch tower, and along the rest of the curtain wall, a series of slits were cut into the defences to enable the castle's defenders to fire on any enemy. These slits were incorporated in all the curtain walls with the exception of the south aspect where the location of the castle was clearly felt to render such defensive features unnecessary.

Along the rest of the north curtain wall the castle's defensive arrangements have now been obscured by the incorporation of more modern *domestic offices*. The line of the original curtain wall is now obliterated by

The watchtower.

Interior north wall of Courtyard.

these buildings. These new domestic apartments were probably built by Sir Rhys ap Thomas in the reign of Henry VII and their construction was doubtless prompted by the desire for more sumptuous accommodation than had been previously included in the twelfth century castle. That these new state apartments were grouped along the castle's northern curtain was an extraordinary arrangement however, even in the more settled period of the fifteenth century. The domestic buildings were placed on the side of the castle most liable to attack and they were further isolated from the castle's main defences on the opposite side of the courtyard.

The *main hall* was situated between the north-west tower and the north curtain watch tower. Evidence of a fireplace in the middle of this section of curtain wall supports this view. A second major fireplace in the large structure next to the watch tower, indicates that this building housed the main *sleeping chambers* of Dinefwr Castle. This structure is some thirteen metres long and ten metres high. Access to both these buildings was through a porch, two metres wide and four metres high, which led from the castle courtyard into the two buildings. Some domestic buildings were also contained in the *south* curtain wall however. A private apartment seems to have been constructed over the castle's main entrance although this could have been Dinefwr's *chapel*. Its windows command extensive views over the surrounding countryside.

It should also be noted that the *garderobe arrangements* (toilet facilities) in Dinefwr were usually complete, there being no fewer than three ranges of garderobes in the south, north-west and north curtain walls.

On the north-eastern approach to Dinefwr can be seen one of the castle's most distinctive features; its large and impressive *keep*. The inclusion of the keep would have necessitated the demolition of the castle's former north and eastern curtain walls and the remains of these walls can be clearly seen at this point. The dressed butt of the east curtain and the position of the rock at this point suggests that the keep was not detached from the courtyard but that an archway connected it with the east wall and a curtain with the northern wall.

The keep at Dinefwr is cylindrical. Cylindrical keeps were introduced into Britain from France late in the twelfth century and possessed clear advantages over the square towers that preceded them. The salient angles of square towers were open to destruction, the corner stones could be removed without difficulty and the defenders, moreover, could not command those angles. The cylindrical keep, in contrast, offered no dead angles while the masonry was less open to damage from the battering-ram or the boring-machine. Cylindrical keeps also provided a wider field of fire.

The precise date of the construction of Dinefwr's keep is unknown, though it was certainly there in 1213 as Rhys Grug and his garrison took refuge in the keep when the rest of the castle fell to his younger relation, Rhys Ieuanc.[2]

The keep at Dinefwr was entered from basement level. There was no internal staircase so communication between floors was probably by trap doors and from wall-walks along the ramparts. An external stairway was added later but that was a comparatively late arrangement, and was certainly not present when the castle was in active use.

Dinefwr's keep contained three apartments, the uppermost once again being of relatively modern construction. This uppermost apartment contains six large windows, each some two metres high, one and a half metres wide and one metre deep, a fireplace and also a doorway connecting with the rampart. This top storey of the keep was probably built in the late seventeenth century and would have served as a summerhouse. Originally it was crowned with a small tower-shaped roof. This feature is clearly shown in Buck's view of 1740 though the roof has long since disappeared. This summerhouse is one of the great castle's most incongruous modern additions. The *Second chamber* in the keep contained a fireplace and two recesses and a chimney but there are no windows in this second storey.

[2] ('Thus did he (the younger Rhys) possess himself of the castle altogether save one tower and in that the garrison secured themselves in fighting and defending with missiles and engines. And outside were the archers and crossbowmen and miners and horsemen fighting against them. And they were compelled before the afternoon to surrender the castle'.) *Brut y Tywysogion*, 1213.

Solar window, north w

Dinefwr's twelfth century keep and domestic buildings.

The *lower storey* is eight metres in diameter and may have been Dinefwr's dungeon. It housed three openings standing some two metres from the level of the courtyard. These **openings were two metres high and one and a** half metres wide with shallow steps leading to the courtyard. Square apertures the length and breadth of the keep provided firing points for archers and, later, gunners.

At its most active, Dinefwr housed a complement of eight thousand warriors (under Pain de Cadurcis) although its more usual complement would have been around two hundred.

The design of Dinefwr Castle offers a fasci-nating insight into the various uses to which castles have been placed over the last thousand years. Beginning with the most primitive and basic castle design, Dinefwr subsequently incorporated all the major developments in defensive design including the revolutionary innovations imported from **the continent in the late twelfth century.** Dinefwr also includes some of the more sophisticated domestic arrangements to be seen in Welsh castles. The present ruin offers intriguing evidence of the lives—both active and domestic—of its many and varied inhabitants.

SELECTED BIBLIOGRAPHY

Archaeologia Cambrensis (1851).

Archaeologia Cambrensis (1925).

Historical Society West Wales, (Vols. I and II).

Hughes, Lynn, *Dear Dynevor . . . An Essay Presented to Lord Dynevor* (1977).

Lloyd, J. E., *History of Carmarthenshire* (1935).

Reid, Alan, *The Castles of Wales* (1973).

Royal Commission on the Ancient and Historical Monuments and Constructions in Wales and Monmouthshire: *An Inventory of the Ancient Monuments in Wales and Monmouthshire, V. The County of Carmarthen* (1917).

Samuel, William, *Llandeilo Past and Present* (1868).

Thomas, Roger, *Castles in Wales* (1982).